What is Medical Education Research?

Katherine A. Moreau and Kaylee Eady

What is Medical Education Research?
Copyright © 2023 by Katherine A. Moreau and Kaylee Eady

Tellwell Talent
www.tellwell.ca

ISBN
978-0-2288-9030-0 (Hardcover)
978-0-2288-9029-4 (Paperback)

About the Authors

Katherine A. Moreau and Kaylee Eady are professors of Health Professions Education in the Faculty of Education at the University of Ottawa and researchers at the Centre for Research on Educational and Community Services at the University of Ottawa.

A new book arrived at the library. It looked around to see where it belonged, but it was perplexed.

Where did it belong? All the other books knew where they belonged in the library, but New Book did not.
Introduction to Medical Education Research
R737
ML410

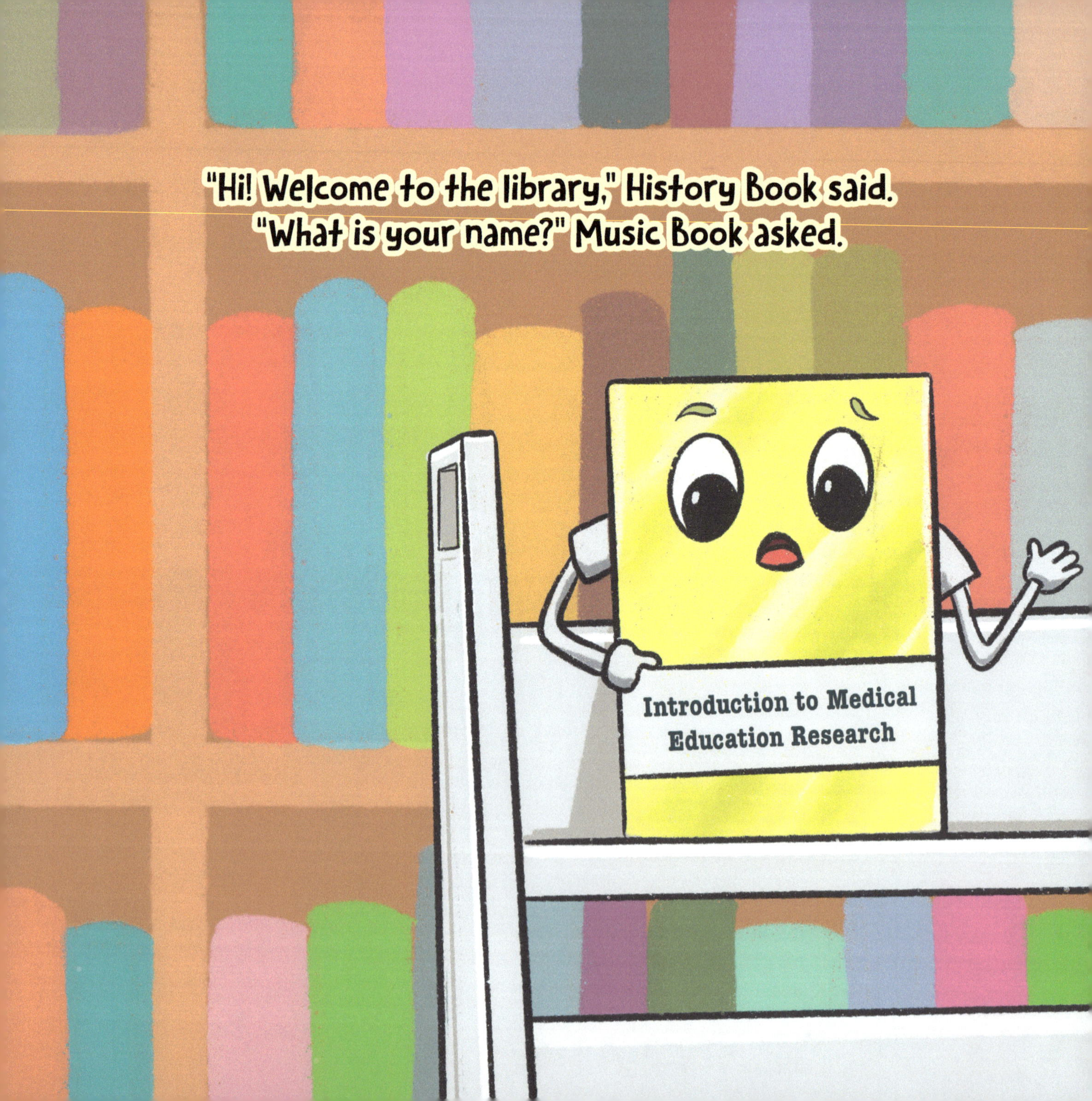

"Hi! Welcome to the library," History Book said.
"What is your name?" Music Book asked.
Introduction to Medical
Education Research

New Book answered, "Hi, my name is Introduction to Medical Education Research."

When History Book and Music Book asked where New Book would live in the library, it replied, "I have no clue! I just don't know."
Introduction to Medical Education Research
R737

"Well, what is medical education research?" History Book inquired.

"Yes, tell us what is on your pages, and we will help you figure out what section you belong in!" Music Book sang.

New Book was thankful for the help. "Okay. Part 1 focuses on what topics are studied in medical education research."

"Tell us the topics," chanted Music Book.

Assesment: Geoffrey Norman

Simulation and Technology-Enhanced Learning: Yvonne Steinert

Competency-Based Medical Education: Jason R. Frank & Olle ten Cate

Medical School Selection:
Kevin Eva

Workplace-Based L...
Ronald M. Harden

"Assessment, Simulation and Technology-Enhanced Learning, Competency-Based Medical Education, Equity, Diversity, and Inclusion, Professional Identity Formation, Continuing Professional Development, Curriculum Development and Program Evaluation, Medical School Selection, Workplace-Based Learning, Interprofessional Education, Physician Wellness and Burnout, Clinical Reasoning, Social Accountability."

"Wow," said History Book. "Medical education research covers a lot of topics. You could belong in a lot of sections of the library. That information does not help us figure out where you belong."

Looking disappointed, New Book continued to flip through its pages to Part 2.

medical education
MEDICAL TEACHER
Part 2 was called "Medical education research: why do it?" New Book skimmed its sentences and read, "People do medical education research to improve the education of healthcare providers so that they can develop their abilities to provide quality care to individuals and populations."
ML410

"Perfect. Then you belong in the Medicine section," History Book proudly announced.

"No, I think you belong in the Education section!" Music Book bellowed.

"We need more clarity," New Book sighed. It moved on to Part 3.

"Who conducts medical education research?" New Book read on to answer the question. "Leaders in medical schools, directors of medical education programs, medical students, residents, physicians, researchers with backgrounds in Education, Psychology, Sociology..."

The list was too long to read in full.

AAMC
PROFESSOR
amee
SCIENTIST/
RESEARCHER
ASME
METHODOLOGIST
ICRE
CIFR
PhD
MD

first author
et al.,
senior author
themes emerge
thematic
ML410

"Well, that is not helpful at all; you could go in all kinds of sections!" proclaimed History Book.

Still confused, New Book went to its fourth and final part, which focused on how to do medical education research. This section was really long. There were many ways to do medical education research, New Book thought.

So New Book summarized. "Medical education research can be done with large teams, small teams, or teams made up of people who have similar or different training. It can also be done using numbers or words or both. There really is not one way of doing it!"

"You have shown us how unique and complex medical education research is," History Book reported, "but I still don't know where you belong in the library."

"I am unique," New Book realized.

the librarian arrived to open the library. the
books went quiet and watched carefully.

the librarian picked up New Book,
flipped through its pages, and headed
for the Medicine section.

R - Medicine
New Book was happy to find its place in the library, but it is still unsure to this day if it belongs solely in the Medicine section.

Hi, I am Researching Medical Education
Hello, I am Survey Methods for Medical and Health Professions Education: A Six-Step Approach
R737

Notes

Notes